9 LESSONS
IN BREXIT

9 LESSONS
IN BREXIT

IVAN ROGERS

Published in 2019 by Short Books,
Unit 316, ScreenWorks, 22 Highbury Grove,
London, N5 2ER

10 9 8 7 6 5 4

ISBN: 978-1-78072-399-0

Cover design by Two Associates

Printed at CPI Group (UK) Ltd, Croydon, CR0 4YY

Introduction

The stakes in the Brexit process could not be higher now. We face the gravest political crisis for at least a couple of generations. The risks are both a democratic crisis and an economic one.

As a former senior civil servant – I was Britain's ambassador to the EU until I resigned my post in January 2017 – I had a long career serving governments of all colours, mostly on international and financial issues.

I am not a politician and have never wanted to be one, and my roles rarely involved speaking publicly. Since leaving Brussels, however, what I have done is to give testimony to several parliamentary committees when they have asked me to do so, and to give lectures at a number of British universities who have invited me to speak about the implications of Brexit, and the real choices we have after leaving the EU. In these interventions I have attempted to bring evidence into a heated argument, in which evidence has all too frequently gone missing.

I am all for rumbustuous debate. Any healthy democracy needs it, and benefits from a serious contest of visions as to its future direction. Part of the problem the European Union has is that the public in several countries, not just the UK, think that too many issues which are central to their own sense of their identity are being dealt with, often by unaccountable people, in ways which they think remove their right to make real choices to change political direction.

But debates about fundamental questions of direction need to be anchored in facts, not fantasies. And ours has suffered since the referendum from a surfeit of the latter, from a near total inability to understand the interests, incentives and motives of the people with whom we are negotiating a divorce, and from what I think are highly unrealistic assessments of the potential national options ahead.

This book is an edited version of the university lecture which has resonated most widely. It offers the nine lessons that I believe we need to draw from the last two and a half years, if the next two and a half – indeed the next decade – are not to be even more painful.

We cannot go on as we have been: evading and obfuscating choices – indeed frequently denying, against all evidence, that there are unavoidable choices. And the public will, understandably, not, for a very long time, forgive a political class which, on all sides of the divide, fails to level with it on the choices being made.

I wish I could say that I thought these nine lessons were in the process of being digested. Perhaps we do at least have some signs that a genuine debate about types of post-Brexit destinations, based on something other than complete wishful thinking, is belatedly breaking out.

But the debate in this country – on all sides – continues to suffer from all manner of delusions, fantasies and self-deceptions.

And the debate in the EU on the British question, insofar as there is one, suffers from complacency, fatigue and strategic myopia.

We are in a bad way. And a descent into a deeply troubled and essentially conflictual medium-term relationship with the EU, and a generation of deeply divided British politics, becomes completely inevitable unless we learn these lessons and apply that learning in the next few years.

So here are nine lessons we need, I think, to learn from the last few years, and the conclusions we need to draw from them.

Ist lesson:

It has of course to be that "Brexit means Brexit".

I do not mean this facetiously. Well, not primarily, anyway… I mean that leaving the EU is genuinely a major regime change, with massive political, legal, economic and social consequences.

Being just outside the EU perimeter fence – even if that is where we choose to be (which I rather doubt) – is not *at all* similar to living just inside it, which is where David Cameron sought to entrench the UK, that is to say, outside political, monetary, banking, fiscal union, outside Schengen (the zone which has abolished passport and all other types of border control), and with a pick-and-choose approach to what used to be the third pillar of justice and home affairs. His was the last attempt to amplify and entrench British exceptionalism *within* the EU legal order.

It failed. A majority voted to leave altogether.

And when they did, they were not told that, at the end of the withdrawal phase of the negotiation, there would be another vote on whether they meant it, once they saw the terms. We can't rewrite the history of what happened.

Incidentally, second vote campaigners seem either remarkably coy about whether they want to remain on the terms Cameron negotiated or whether some great new offer will be forthcoming – notably on free movement of people – from EU elites supposedly desperate to give us something now which they were not prepared to give to Cameron.

So let me puncture that fantasy first: no such offer will be coming.

If we stayed, we could, contrary to what some allege, keep the existing membership terms.

But that includes no promise of improving them. I have yet to meet, for example, the senior person in any capital who wants to give Member States the right to impose numerical controls on free movement rights.

And this is because, among the other 27 Member States, without exception, free movement is not at all the same business as external migration.

Their crisis – which is severe and extremely difficult to handle – is about external migration. And for them, the British response to that crisis from both the last two Prime Ministers – has essentially been: we have an opt-out from any joint action on that one. What you 27 do via common policies is up to you. We'll help out with aid in the affected regions.

It still amazes me that virtually the entire British political class still thinks that its free movement preoccupations are shared in the 27.

They aren't.

To come back to the fundamental choice, though, once you have decided to leave the EU, you cannot, from just outside the fence, achieve all the benefits you got when just inside it.

First, there will, under *no* circumstances, be frictionless trade when outside the Single Market and Customs Union. Frictionless trade comes with free movement of people. And with the European Court of Justice. More later on that.

Second, voluntary alignment from outside – i.e. a sovereign UK decision to copy the EU's rules into our own law book – even where that makes sense or is frankly just inevitable – does *not* deliver all the benefits of membership. Because, unlike members, you are not subject to the adjudication and enforcement machinery to which all members are.

And that's what Brexiteers wanted, right? British laws and British Courts. Not supranational laws and a "foreign" court.

Fine. But then market access into what is now *their* market, governed by supranational laws and courts of which you are no longer part – and not, as it used to be, yours – is worse and more limited than before.

That is unavoidable. It is not vindictive, voluntary, a punishment beating, or any of the other nonsense we hear daily. It is just ineluctable reality.

And finally, the solidarity of the club members will *always* be with each other, not with you. We have seen that over the backstop issue during the last 18 months. The 26 supported Dublin, not London. They still do. Nothing the Prime Minister now bids for will change that.

This may be the first Anglo-Irish negotiation in history where the greater leverage is not on London's side of the table. And the vituperation aimed at Dublin politicians tells one just how well that has gone down with politicians and apparatchiks who had not bothered to work out that this was no longer just a bilateral business, and are now appalled to find they are cornered.

Well, just wait till the trade negotiations. When these take place, the solidarity of the remaining Member States will be with the major fishing Member States, not with the UK. The solidarity will be with Spain, not the UK, when Madrid makes Gibraltar-related demands in the trade negotiation endgame. The solidarity will be with Cyprus when it says it wants to avoid precedents which might be applied to Turkey.

I could go on. And on... The Free Trade Agreement talks will be tougher than anything we have seen to date.

Even now, UK politicians, including former Conservative leaders and Foreign Secretaries, really seem to think – they even write it – that if we just asserted ourselves more aggressively in negotiations, a typical multi-day, multi-night summit would deliver them some fundamentally different EU offer.

But the EU is negotiating with us, not as a member, but as a prospective soon-to-be third country. Those glorious, sweaty, fudge-filled Brussels denouements are gone. The Prime Minister is not in a room negotiating with the 27. That's not how the exit game or the trade negotiation works, or was ever going to.

We need, urgently, on all sides of the spectrum, to start understanding how being a "third country" is different. And the most naïve of all on this issue remain the Brexiteers who fantasise about a style of negotiation which is only open to members of the club.

We are indeed, a soon-to-be third country and, to a significant extent, an opponent and rival, not just a partner, now. Again, that is what Brexit advocates argued for. They do not want to be a partner in a project the objectives of which they mostly disagree with.

It is time to accept the consequences.

Some of those will be beyond tiresome. And one of them will be that we shall be, like Switzerland, in a state of permanent negotiations with the EU about something highly intractable, on which they may have more metaphorical tanks than us.

Get used to it!

2ND LESSON:

Other people have sovereignty too. And they too may choose to "take back control" of things you would rather they didn't.

The sovereigntist argument for Brexit, which was one powerful element of the referendum campaign – taking back control of laws, borders and money – is a perfectly legitimate case to make.

If you think the consequences of living in a bloc where the pooling of sovereignty has gone well beyond the technical regulatory domain into huge areas of public life are intolerable for democratic legitimacy and accountability, that is a more than honourable position.

But others who have chosen to pool their sovereignty in ways and to extents which make you feel uncomfortable with the whole direction of the project, have done so because they believe pooling *enhances* their sovereignty – in the sense of adding to their "power of agency" in a world order in which modestly sized nation states have relatively little say – rather than diminishing it.

They did not want that pooling to stop at the purely technical trade and regulatory domain.

Brexit advocates may think this is a fundamental historical error, and has led to overreach by the questionably accountable supranational institutions of their club. They may think that it leads to legislation, opaquely agreed by often unknown legislators, which unduly favours heavyweight incumbent lobbyists.

Fine. There is some justice in much of this critique.

Then leave the club. But you cannot, in the act of leaving it, expect the club fundamentally to redesign its founding principles to suit you and to share its sovereignty with you when it still suits you, and to dilute their agency in so doing.

It simply is not going to. And both Her Majesty's Government and Brexit advocates outside it seem constantly to find this frustrating, vexatious and some kind of indication of EU ill will.

We have seen this in both former Brexit Secretaries' conceptions of how deep mutual recognition agreements should be offered to the UK, alone of all "third countries" with which the EU deals, and in the initial propositions on both financial services, other services and data.

We saw it with the bizarre – and total non-starter – Schroedinger's Customs Union Facilitated Customs Arrangement proposal of the PM which was central to her Chequers proposal in summer 2018, whereby we got all the benefits of staying in a Customs Union with the EU whilst leaving it to have a fully sovereign trade policy.

We see it in the constant "have your cake and eat it" demands which run through every document the European Research Group produce or endorse. And we even see it in the railing against the "subordination to inflexible pooled law of the EU" which, in Richard Dearlove's and others' view, is what the Prime Minister is prepared to sign up to in her proposed deal and which they see as intolerable on national security grounds.

But if by sovereignty we mean more than purely nominal decision-making power and we mean something about the genuine projection of the UK's power in a world where autarky – ie. complete economic self-sufficiency – mercifully is not an option, then, as we get into the deeper trade, economic and security negotiations ahead, we are going to need a far more serious national debate about trade-offs.

And the trade-offs are real and difficult. No one should pretend that all the answers will be great.

To take just one technical example (though it rapidly develops a national security as well as an economic dimension): cross border data flows are now completely central to free trade and prosperity. Not that you would know it from listening to our current trade debate, which remains bizarrely obsessed with tariffs which, outside agriculture, have become a very modest element in the real barriers to cross border trade.

The EU here is a global player – a global rule maker – able and willing effectively to impose its values, rules and standards extraterritorially.

Before the referendum, we had Brexit-supporting senior ministers and advisers, who should have known better, fantasising about the autonomy we would have to plough our own furrow once sovereignty had been resumed and we were no longer obliged to live under the jackboot of the General Data Protection Regulation (GDPR) – the huge piece of EU legislation, which, as of this May, governs data issues across the whole EU including us.

Sobriety only started to set in in this debate after the referendum, as the implications of a failure on the UK's part to achieve a so-called "adequacy determination" from the EU under GDPR – in other words, a formal agreement from the EU that the UK's own rules and standards would be equivalent in their effects to the EU's, and therefore not cause barriers to be erected – started to become clear. And this only because corporates across a huge range of sectors started to spell out those implications for ministers.

But it goes well beyond corporates. Ministers start now to understand that the value of the national security exemption in Article 4.2 of the Treaty on the European Union might have been much easier to defend and enforce as a member of the EU, than it will be from outside.

The same applies to so-called "equivalence decisions" in masses of financial sector legislation – on which the EU decides, in sovereign fashion, whether the rules in "third countries" achieve outcomes sufficiently close to their own, to enable them to offer better market access to the firms of those countries than reliance on simple World Trade Organisation rules would dictate.

Again, the consequences of failure to achieve such decisions will be the very substantial erosion of access into EU markets by UK companies.

What, really, are these "equivalence" and "adequacy" stories about? They are the EU projecting power – which it does quite as well as, and probably more effectively than, Washington, in multiple critical regulatory areas – and using its pooling of *internal* sovereignty to impose its values and standards well beyond its borders.

"Going global", unless it's purely an empty slogan, is precisely the ability to project both force and influence beyond one's borders.

Why does the current UK debate on sovereignty leave so many corporate players mystified and cold – and I am not, incidentally, for one minute saying such views outweigh others'?

Because in "taking back control" over our laws and leaving the adjudication and enforcement machinery of what used to be our "home" market, we are privileging notional autonomy to make our own laws over real power to set the rules by which in practice we shall be governed, since departure from norms set by others when we are not in the room will in practice greatly constrain our room for manoeuvre.

The massive costs of deviation will force large-scale compliance with rules set without our input or involvement.

The EU will decide, on sovereignty and fiscal stability grounds, that it is intolerable for certain kinds of activity to take place completely outside its jurisdiction. We may hate this intransigence, and in many instances, it may indeed be both unnecessary and unwise. What, from the outside, though, can we do about it?

We shall, in practice, struggle to achieve even observer status in the setting of policies which will have a major impact on our national life.

In the next few years, we have to have these debates, openly and seriously, or the public will soon conclude that much of the supposed control they won back was just a simulacrum of sovereignty for some empty suits in Westminster, with the real decisions about their lives still taken elsewhere.

That will not end well for some of the right honourable members for the 18th century.

3RD LESSON:

Brexit is a process not an event. And the EU, while strategically myopic, is formidably good at process against negotiating opponents. We have to be equally so, or we will get hammered. Repeatedly.

One cannot seriously simultaneously advance the arguments that the EU has morphed away from the common market we joined, and got into virtually every nook and cranny of UK life, eroding sovereignty across whole tracts of the economy, internal and external security, *and* that we can extricate ourselves from all that in a trice, recapture our sovereignty and rebuild the capability of the UK state to govern and regulate itself in vast areas where it has surrendered sovereignty over the previous 45 years. The people, who three years ago said that you could, were simply not serious. And they have proven it. They also had not the slightest fag packet plan on what they were going to try and do and in which order.

Bold, confident assertions, during and in the many months after the referendum, that we would have a fully fledged trade deal with the EU ready and in force by the day of exit, and, not only that, rafts of further free trade deals with other fast-growing countries across the globe, were just risible when they were made, and have now proven empty bluster.

The same goes for all the breezy assertions that "no deal" would pose no great problems for aviation, for road haulage, for medicines, for food, for financial services, for data and for any number of other areas – for most of which, "WTO terms" are simply not a safety harness.

No number of repetitions of the grossly misleading term "WTO deal" makes it any more real or effective. Its proponents – or most of them – know this full well, incidentally.

I say this not as an agent of Establishment remainer sabotage. But because these assertions were always fantasies, produced by people who, at the point they uttered them, would not have known a "trade treaty" if they had found one in their soup.

What we needed to do very early on was to recognise the complexity and inevitable longevity of the exit process, work out our viable options, achieve real clarity about where we wanted to land, having worked honestly through the very tough choices we faced – and still do face – and reconcile ourselves to a serious period of transition.

And also to recognise that there could never,

on the part of the remaining Member States, be the appetite to have *two* tortuous negotiations with the UK – one to deliver a few years of a transition/bridging deal, the other to agree the end state after exit. One such negotiation is enough for everyone. So transitional arrangements were always going to be "off the shelf".

Put bluntly, neither of these points was recognised. Instead, before much of the serious work to look at where we wanted to land post exit had happened, we locked ourselves into a fixed date for the invocation of Article 50.

That duly forfeited at a stroke any leverage over how that process would run. And it handed the 27, who had, by the morning of June 24th 2016, already set out their "no negotiation without (Article 50) notification" position, the first couple of goals of the match in the opening five minutes.

All the people who are now loudest in bemoaning the Prime Minister's deal were, of course, the loudest in cheering from the rafters as she made this fateful error.

Many are now hastily rewriting history to claim they were always against it. They weren't, though. I remember it rather well.

"Brussels" is nothing if not really expert at using the tensions in domestic national politics to force the moves it most wants you to make.

People there were just quietly amused with the adulation the Prime Minister duly got for walking straight into the trap.

One really cannot blame the 27 for playing it as they did. Though one can and should blame them for having had too few serious top level discussions themselves about the relationship with the UK working after exit.

Before the Prime Minister had even turned up for her first ever leaders' meeting, the combination of that decision to guarantee notification by a certain date and the red lines substance of her first party conference leader's speech had completely cemented the solidarity of the 27 – which has held soundly ever since – on how to kick off and to design the sequencing of the process which has led to where we are today.

It's about the only first-order issue since 2016 on which the EU27 have since held together in near perfect harmony. If that does not tell you something about this government's negotiating prowess, what will?

Anyone who understood the dynamic could read it all in the European Council Conclusions in June, October and December of 2016, and in the words of key EU leaders through the autumn of that year.

The party conference speech and the Lancaster House one which followed it were a gift from heaven to those in the EU – who were many – concerned that the UK might be able to divide and rule and introduce internal tensions within the EU.

These speeches were largely for domestic consumption. But, for the subsequent negotiation process, they were, as the saying goes, "worse than a crime; they were a mistake".

For, in the total self-absorption of party conferences and Westminster, no one was paying much attention to how the EU was patiently constructing the process designed to maximise its leverage.

Even by April 2017, when the first set of so-called guidelines emerged from the leaders at 27, it was hard to get anyone here to read them. We were, as usual, preoccupied more with the noises from the noisy but largely irrelevant in Westminster, while the real work was being done on the other side of the Channel.

And yet those very expertly crafted guidelines led completely inexorably to the December 2017 agreement. And the substance of that, in turn, led equally inexorably to all the elements of the Prime Minister's deal which has caused the furore. The battle on sequencing which the then Brexit Secretary (David Davis) declared to be the battle of the summer of 2017, was actually long lost before he started fighting it.

Anyone who expresses their outrage about the outcome only now is either feigning indignation, or was just not paying attention 12, 18 and 24 months ago, when it mattered.

And, because the UK had given no serious thought to the question of transitional arrangements until it was too late – due to the fantasies propagated that this would be one of the "easiest trade deals in human history" and all would be definitively tied up legally by exit day – by the time they actually did focus, London was urgently begging for what is now pejoratively termed the "vassal state" transition. Precisely because it knew that it could not be ready for a post-Brexit equilibrium state by March 2019.

All the EU had to do was to ensure that the

transition hinged off a Withdrawal Treaty containing a permanent legal all-weather backstop, and it knew that the UK had no alternative but to sign such a Withdrawal Agreement.

No amount of bold, but empty, talk about "no deal" being "better than a bad deal", however oft repeated at whatever level of government, made the slightest difference to the 27's assessment of the negotiating reality: the UK needed much more time, and failure to get it would be much worse for it than all alternatives.

As I have said before, I am all for knowing your "Best Alternative To a Negotiated Deal" – your BATNA – in negotiations. You have to know whether you can walk out, and be very sure you understand what could happen if you do, and what you can do to mitigate all downsides.

But, if you are emitting all sorts of signals which indicate that you know you cannot, don't bluff. It just makes you look weak, not strong, and it fools no one.

Those who were suckered into doing, or cheering, the wrong thing in the negotiation at the wrong time for the wrong reason, and duped themselves and others into thinking it would all be extraordinarily simple, cannot acknowledge that of course.

So the narrative has been of "betrayal" by a remainer elite who sabotaged the "no deal" plans. It is the emerging British equivalent of the Dolchstosslegende – the stab in the back myth – which, post Versailles, the German military, Hindenburg and others, propagated to blame the Weimar civilian elite for having betrayed a supposedly undefeated army.

The fact is, that the efficacy of "no deal" preparations depends massively, as we are now – very belatedly again – hearing, on what others do, not just on UK actions.

And if you set yourself a ludicrous, unachievable deadline for a complete regime change, don't be shocked that others cleverly use the pressure of the clock and the cliff edge to dictate the shape of that change.

It is, in the end, the total absence of a serious realistic plan for the process of Brexit as well as of a serious coherent conception of a post-Brexit destination which has delivered this denouement to stage one of what will be, whether Brexit proponents like it or not, a much longer process.

For the next stage, we need much less self-absorption, a vastly clearer, less self-deceiving understanding of the incentives on the other side of the table, and a less passive approach to the construction of the process. We need serious substance not plausible bullshit.

We already see in the Withdrawal Agreement the clear signs that, having succeeded with its negotiating plans in this phase, the EU will repeat the clock and cliff edge pressures in the run up the next UK election, knowing that it can and will exact concessions as the deadline looms. But walking away to a "no deal" outcome, managed or not, does not escape that pressure.

One can, of course, blame the EU for over-doing their success in ordering the whole negotiations, though this has rather the flavour of blaming Mo Salah for banging in a hat-trick and not stopping at two.

Has EU tactical negotiating acumen turned into a strategically myopic blunder because they have over-egged it and won the first leg too emphatically? Or can our brave lads recover in the second leg if only they are finally led by a boss who just has enough "belief"?

I think the football metaphors are best stopped there. Except to say that I thought the days when we had persuaded ourselves that we would win a tournament if we could just exhibit more "passion" than the opponents had gone.

It really helps, in a negotiation, actually to know what you are doing and be stone-cold sober about the real interests of the other players.

4TH LESSON:

It is not possible or democratic to argue (as hard Brexiteers do) that only one Brexit destination is true, legitimate and representative of the revealed "Will of the People" and that all other potential destinations outside the EU are "Brexit in Name Only".

The public voted in the referendum – in huge numbers – and the majority voted to "leave" and not to "remain". That much is clear. But people were not asked to give their reasons for voting "leave" or "remain", and they were multifarious on both sides.

For decades, some of the staunchest standard bearers of the case for leaving the post-Maastricht Treaty EU have made the case for staying in the so-called Single Market, remaining a signatory to the EEA Agreement but leaving the institutions of political and juridical integration of the Union.

I have spent years reading Eurosceptic tomes – plenty of them very well argued, whether you agree with them or not – arguing that Maastricht, amplified by subsequent Treaties, represented the wrong turn in European integration, and that what we needed to do was to return to the essential mercantile ideas behind the internal market project and jettison UK adherence to the rest.

For many people I have talked to, especially outside the metropolitan elite circles who obsess about post-Brexit models, that sense of "we only ever joined a Common Market, but it's turned into something very different and no one in authority down in London ever asked us whether that is what we wanted" is probably the closest to capturing their reasons for voting "leave".

One can't now suddenly start denouncing people who advocate staying in a Common Market-type relationship with the EU as Quisling closet remainers who do not subscribe to the "only true path" Brexit. Let alone insist on public self-criticism from several senior politicians on the Right, from Nigel Farage to Dan Hannan, via many other Conservative front benchers, who themselves, within the last few years, have publicly praised the Norwegian and Swiss models, the health of their democracies and their prosperity outside the EU.

Saying now that ending up with a Norwegian or Swiss-style deal would represent a "Brexit in Name Only" betrayal of the "Will of the People" must indicate that one believes that when the Norwegian and Swiss people voted – as they did – not to join the EU, and take a very different path outside it, they in fact voted for something worse than EU membership. And are not the proud, sovereign, successful nations most Brexiteers told us, before the referendum, that they were.

Before the referendum, these were countries trumpeted by Brexiters as having essentially rejected European political integration in favour of vibrant democracy.

But now we are effectively being told their democracy is not a real one, because their chosen course leaves them still far too integrated into EU institutions and rules.

You cannot credibly, within a three-year period, argue diametrically opposite cases.

In another lecture, I described Brexitism as a revolutionary phenomenon, which radicalised as time went on and was now devouring its own children. This current phase feels ever more like Maoists seeking to crush Rightist deviationists than it does British Conservatism.

To be clear, I am not making an argument here for a UK version of an EEA model (a Norwegian-style deal, involving adherence to Single Market legislation), as opposed to the current proposed deal. I have no time in this book to rehearse the arguments either for or against this potential version of Brexit. I have plenty of reservations about the merits for the UK of an EEA destination, dating from my Treasury days.

That said, I have just as many reservations with the Prime Minister's proposed deal. I also deplore the way in which the substance of all the models is constantly distorted by those who do not understand them – opponents and proponents – and who have then given them a few days' thought, in a panic.

My real objection is to the style of argument espoused both by the pro "no deal" Right and by Downing Street which says that no other model but their own is a potentially legitimate interpretation of the Will of the People – which evidently only they can properly discern.

Both fervent leavers and fervent remainers as well as No 10 seem to me now to seek to delegitimise *a priori* every version of the world they don't support.

As for the Prime Minister's proposed model, the entire EU knows that where we have now reached derives from her putting the ending of free movement of people well above all other objectives, and privileging as near frictionless trade in goods as she can get over the interests of UK services sectors.

They are unsurprised by the former but surprised – sometimes gleefully – by the latter, as it seems to point directly to a deal skewed in their favour, because they have a huge trade surplus in goods, whereas we have the major surplus in services.

We have essentially sacrificed all ambition on services sectors in return for ending free movement, sold the latter as a boon (when amongst other things, it clearly diminishes the value of a UK passport), and presented the former as a regaining of sovereignty, when it guarantees a major loss of market access in by far our largest export market.

Well, by all means argue for that. I fully accept that control of borders – albeit with a lot of confusion about the bit we already have complete control over, namely, migration from outside the EU (on which nothing effective to bring those numbers down to meet the Government's own targets has been delivered) – was a central referendum issue.

But don't argue that it's the only feasible Brexit. Or that it's an economically rational, let alone optimal, one.

Of course the EU side will now back the Prime Minister in saying it is. They have done a great deal for themselves and they want it to stick. Who can blame them?

5TH LESSON:

If WTO terms or existing EU preferential deals are not good enough for the UK in major "third country" markets, they can't be good enough for trade with our largest market.

You cannot simultaneously argue that it is perfectly fine to leave a deep free trade agreement with easily our largest export and import market for the next generation, and trade solely on WTO terms because that is how we and others trade with everyone else... *and* argue that it is imperative we get out of the EU in order that we can strike preferential trade deals with large parts of the rest of the world, because the existing terms on which we trade with the rest of the world are intolerable.

If moving beyond WTO terms with major markets represents a major step *forward* in liberalising trade, then deliberately moving back to WTO terms from an existing deep preferential agreement – which is what the Single Market is – represents a major step *backward* to less free trade. You really can't have it both ways.

I say "you cannot" argue this, but clearly many can and do. It is beyond incoherent.

It is fine and legitimate to argue that the UK should aim at a global lattice-work of bilateral and plurilateral free trade deals – especially in the current absence of an ability to drive forward major multilateral trade liberalisation through the WTO at a time when the US has manifestly ceased to be interested in it, and may indeed be setting about deliberalising trade, undermining the organisation and regretting having allowed China into it.

It is equally legitimate to argue, as I mentioned earlier, that you only want free trade deals which stop well short of the intrusion on national sovereignty, which Single Market harmonisation and mutual recognition via supranational legislation, adjudication and enforcement entails. As long as you *also* recognise that all trade deals inevitably erode and trammel one's sovereignty to some degree – often to a significant degree.

If you make binding international commitments to opening your markets – on goods, services, government procurement, whatever – in return for other states making equally binding commitments, which open up opportunities for your firms in their markets, that seriously limits your capacity to regulate sectors of the economy as you might ideally see fit.

Genuinely free global trade actually seriously trammels national sovereignty. That's why the old advocates of "socialism in one country" were never keen on trade liberalisation, whether in multilateral or bilateral deals.

Indeed, the greatest reason to be a passionate free trader – which I am – is surely that: it curtails the ability of myopic politicians to erect barriers to commerce in the name of sovereignty and national preference against non-national producers.

This is why our current debate on sovereignty and "taking back control" is often frankly so bizarre. It is just comical listening to right-wing populist politicians claiming they are avid free traders and simultaneously saying that one of the purposes of taking back control is to be able to rig domestic markets/competitions in favour of British suppliers/producers.

Protectionism is always someone else's sin, of course.

And the Tory Party has been through these – decades-long – spasms before. Joseph Chamberlain's Tariff Reform and Imperial Preference campaign, as loudly pious, nationalist and messianic as many today, led all the way through to his son Neville's protectionist legislation of the early 1930s which helped worsen a post-financial crisis economy. Sound familiar?

A post-Brexit Britain which is committed to openness and free trade will need first of all to run hard to stand still, as two thirds of UK exports are currently either to the EU or to countries with whom the EU has a preferential trade deal, which we shall first have to try and roll over.

Market access into the EU *will* worsen, whatever post-exit deal we eventually strike. And the quantum by which our trade flows with the EU will diminish – and that will hit immediately after exit – will outweigh the economic impact of greater market opening which we have to aim to achieve over time in other markets. The benefits of those trade deals will not be immediate but incremental over a decade or two.

As the country debates its future trade policy in the next stage of negotiations both with the EU and with other markets it needs honesty from politicians that trade agreements take a long time; that even if every deal we aspire to were completed, this will have a very modest impact on overall UK economic performance. (Good trade deals are worth doing, but there is no serious evidence suggesting that such deals alone could have a transformative effect on UK economic performance.)

And that every version of Brexit involves a worsening of the UK's trade position and a loss of market access to its largest market. As we strive to limit the extent of that worsening and loss, public debate will have to be serious about what the real trade-offs are. Because the EU will be quite brutal in teaching us them.

Meanwhile, before we have even left, we have seen, in the last two and a half years, the most anaemic boost to UK net trade triggered by *any* major sterling devaluation since the Second World War. For politicians not completely blinded by their own rhetoric, the warning signs for the UK economy as we worsen our trade terms with the Continent are there to see. Again, public debate needs to be based on the realities, not on fantasy. Or the reality will soon catch up with us.

6TH LESSON:

The huge problem for the UK with either reversion to WTO terms or with a standard free trade deal with the EU is in services.

This is, perhaps, less a lesson of the last two and a half years than the curious case of the dog that has largely failed to bark so far. But it will bark in the next few years. And again, the public needs to be aware of the big trade-offs that are coming next…or resentment when the next set of climb-downs begins will be off the scale.

So far, both during the referendum and

since, the trade debate has been dominated by trade in goods, tariffs issues and some discussion of the impact on manufacturing supply chains of departing the Single Market and Customs Union.

I don't want to be excessively unkind here, but politicians find goods trade and tariffs more graspable than services trade and the huge complexities of non-tariff barriers in services sectors. They rarely grasp the extent to which goods and services are bundled together and indissociable. They even more rarely grasp how incredibly tough it is to deliver freer cross-border trade in services which, by definition, gets you deep into domestic sovereignty questions in a way which makes removing tariff barriers look easy.

Services sectors represent over three quarters of our economy. And whilst, self-evidently, plenty of services – hairdressing, for example – are not tradable across borders, many of the things in which the UK has proved globally most competitive for many decades are tradable – financial, business, legal, accountancy, consultancy, and tertiary level education services, to name a few.

UK services exports to the EU in the year of the referendum were running at £90 billion a year. That's as much as we export to our next eight export markets put together.

And politicians even yet more rarely grasp that, however imperfect they think EU attempts at internal cross border services liberalisation, anyone who has negotiated with the US, China, India, Japan or sundry others can tell them why far-reaching market-opening services deals, bene- fitting major cross-border services traders, are pretty few and far between. Levels of trust and mutual understanding, and the institutions which are needed to underpin both, have to be very high for services deals to work.

As the Prime Minister gradually backed away from her original red lines, realising that she would imperil large tracts of UK manufacturing if she persisted with it, her position softened on quasi Customs Union propositions. Hence the constant howls of betrayal from those who thought October 2016 and Lancaster House mapped the only true path to Brexit.

Her only way to seek to sell this softening of her position politically – so far with very little sign of success – was to talk boldly about greater autonomy and divergence in services regulation, while she quietly moved towards wanting voluntary permanent alignment of our rules on goods.

The reality, as I say, is that the needs of UK services' industries have been sacrificed to the primary goal of ending free movement.

And post exit, and post the end of any transitional arrangement, it is UK services exporters who will face the starkest worsening of trade terms because of the substantial difference between how relatively liberalised services trade is under even the highly imperfect European services single market and the very best that is achievable under any other form of free trade or regional agreement on the planet.

Yet it is, to repeat, in services sectors where the UK currently has a sizeable trade surplus with the EU, whereas in manufactured goods we have a huge deficit. The interests of some of the most successful sectors of the UK economy over decades are being subordinated to the ending of free movement – under cover of rhetoric that suggests we are becoming more open when we are, in practice, making trade more difficult and less free.

For all the imperfections of the Single Market, services trade between Member States is, in many sectors, freer than it is between the federal states of the US, or the provinces in Canada. The US government is unable, even if it were willing, to deliver on commitments in many areas in international negotiations, just as it cannot bind its states on government procurement, on which many federal states are as protectionist as it gets.

Not that one ever hears a squeak on this from those who rail at EU protectionism.

But the extent and type of cross-border free trade that exists in the Single Market ceases when you leave. A very large proportion of cross-border services trade conducted outside the Single Market only happens because firms have offices physically established in the countries to which they are exporting.

So we know already that cross-border supply will diminish pretty radically post exit, and that the ability to establish legal entities with ease and to conclude ambitious deals on the temporary free movement of workers and on the mutual recognition of qualifications will be central to trying to sustain trade flows in much colder conditions, to limit the impact on the UK economy.

Make no mistake about it, though, a substantial hit on the balance of trade and on the public finances of substantial relocations out of the UK's jurisdiction is guaranteed, because we have rendered the best mode of supplying services across borders far harder. This is consistently ignored, denied or swept under the carpet by those demanding a much more radical so-called "clean break" Brexit. But it will be obvious in the next two years.

The implications are clear. And again the public is not being told of them. Because the fiction has to be maintained – at least until a first deal is done – that there will be no sort of preferential free movement terms for EU citizens.

And so we stagger on, repeatedly postponing

the long promised White Paper on immigration post Brexit, and now, having finally produced it, knowing that once the FTA negotiations truly get under way and reality bites on the UK the policy of removing all preferential treatment for EU citizens, like so many other policies, in the last 30 months, will disintegrate in the face of negotiating imperatives.

The EU is well aware that the UK will, under whoever's premiership, be prepared to pay a heavy price to maintain better access to business, legal, consultancy and financial services markets than other third countries have, to date, achieved via standard FTAs. Why? Because that's an economic imperative for a country which has our world class services capability, and needs market access in much its largest market place.

That EU leverage will be deployed in the years ahead and it will be used to enforce deals on issues like fisheries, on which – again –

certain referendum campaign commitments will be abandoned in the teeth of reality.

Those saying this now will of course get the ritual denunciations for defeatism, lack of belief, treachery and whatever.

But just give it two more years. The Brexiteers, the strength of whose case to the public always resided, as I say, in telling the public that their leaders had mis-sold them on what the EU was becoming, have now done their own mis-selling. And they are in the middle of the painful process of discovering that, as trade terms worsen on exit (which they denied would happen), they will, under economic duress, have to let down the very communities to whom they promised the post Brexit dividend.

That penny is dropping. Just very slowly.

7TH LESSON:

Beware all supposed deals bearing "pluses".

Norway +, Canada +... The "pluses" merely signify that all deficiencies in the named deal will miraculously disappear when we Brits come to negotiate our own version of it.

As the scale of the humiliation which they think the Prime Minister's proposed deal delivers started, far too late, to dawn on politicians who had thought Brexit was a cakewalk – with the emphasis on cake – we have seen a proliferation of mostly half-baked cake alternatives being generated. They all carry at least one +

after the country which represents the alleged template for us. Canada has even acquired several.

Besides "Canada +++" or "Super-Canada", as it was termed by the former Foreign Secretary, we have Norway +, which used to be "Norway-then-Canada" then became "Norway-for-now" and then became "Norway + forever". And now even "No deal +", which also makes appearances as "Managed no deal" and "No deal mini deals".

What is depressing about the nomenclature is the sheer dishonesty. The pluses are inserted to enable one to say that one is well aware of why the existing FTA x or y or European Economic Area deal a or b does not really work as a Brexit destination, but that, with the additions you are proposing, the template is complete and perfect.

We even have the wonderfully preposterous sight of ex-Brexit Secretaries alleging that the very Canada + deal they want has already been offered by Presidents Tusk and Juncker and that all that needs doing is to write this as the destination into the Political Declaration.

But, let me tell you, as someone dealing with both Presidents and their teams at the outset of this process: what the EU Institutions mean by Canada + is not remotely what ex-Brexit and Foreign Secretaries and the Institute of Economic Affairs scribes mean by it. The title page is the same; the contents pages are different.

Not for nothing did an unkind Brussels source label Boris Johnson's "plan A +" (another + of course), Chequers 3.0.

That proposition, is, as he himself might have put it, "an inverted pyramid of piffle". And aside from containing a wish list – an understandable wish list – of things that are not actually present in Canada's EU deal, it does not solve the backstop. Nor does a Norway model, which is why one element of the + is precisely what the Norwegians do not have with the EU: a Customs Union.

"No deal +" is brought to us courtesy of all the people who declared that a great free trade deal would be struck before we even left because the mercantile interests of key manufacturing players in Member States would prevail against the pettifogging legalistic ivory tower instincts of the Brussels ayatollahs.

Forgive me for pointing out that, as some of us forecast well over two years ago, it did not turn out like that. And that the Brussels theologians actually exhibited rather more flexibility than the key Member States when it came to the crunch.

And that not a peep was heard from the titans of corporate Europe, except to back very robustly the position in capitals that the continued integrity of the Single Market project was vastly more important to them than the terms of a framework agreement with the UK. A position which won't change during the trade negotiations ahead either.

The "No deal +" fantasy is that if we just had the guts to walk away, refuse to sign the Withdrawal Agreement with the backstop in it, and withhold a good half of the money the Prime Minister promised this time last year, capitals, suddenly realising we were serious, would come running for a series of mini deals which assured full trading continuity in all key sectors on basically unchanged Single Market and Customs Union terms.

I don't know what tablets these people are taking, but I must confess I wish I were on them. It will be said of them as it was said of the Bourbons, I think: "They have learned nothing and they have forgotten nothing".

The reality is that, if the deal on the table falls apart because we have said "no", there will not be some smooth rapid suite of mini side deals – from aviation to fisheries, from road haulage to data, from derivatives to customs and veterinary checks, from medicines to financial services – as the EU affably sits down with this Prime Minister or another one.

The 27 will legislate and institute unilaterally temporary arrangements which assure continuity where they need it, and cause us asymmetric difficulties where they can. And a UK government, which knows that the efficacy of most of its contingency planning depends, to a greater or lesser degree, on others' actions out of its control, will then have to react – no doubt with a mixture of inevitable compliance and bellicose retaliation.

We already see the next generation of fantasies out there, and it's now just a matter of time before a Tory leadership contender offers them publicly a Houdini act: a suite of very rapid, legal mini deals, accompanied by the existing Withdrawal Agreement deal on citizens' rights, the complete dropping of the backstop, and a requirement only to pay the remainder of the £39 billion cheque when the mini deals have turned into the miraculous Canada (with lots of pluses) deal.

All of which must happen in months. But of course…

To which the EU answer will be a calm but clear "Dream on. You still want a transition? All existing terms and conditions apply. And when it comes to any FTA – deep or shallow – nothing is agreed till everything is agreed – and that still includes the fish."

They may put it slightly more politely. But not much, in the circumstances.

And to anyone who tells me – and we shall assuredly hear plenty of it in the coming months, – "but the EU stands to lose access to London's capital markets and their companies will suffer unless they do our quick and dirty 'no deal' deal", I think I would just say "even the last 30 months have evidently not taught you how the EU functions: try again in another 30…"

If we lurch, despite Parliament evidently wishing to avoid it, towards a "no deal", on the basis it might be "managed" into a quick and dirty FTA, that will not end happily or quickly.

I am in no position to second guess those who have to try and model the macro effects of such a scenario. No developed country has left a trade bloc before, let alone in disorderly fashion, and let alone one which has become a lot more than a trade bloc.

But I do fully understand the legal realities. And because so-called "WTO rules" deliver no continuity in multiple key sectors of the economy, we could expect disruption on a scale and of a length that no one has experienced in the developed world in the last couple of generations.

The complacency that such things cannot

and would not ever really happen in modern economies is staggering. Mercifully, it is not shared in either Whitehall or the Berlaymont.

But these are potential outcomes which proper political leadership is about understanding in huge depth, and knowing whether, regardless of any contingency planning you might do, you believe "no deal" to be, as Cabinet Ministers have recently described it, "disastrous" or "cataclysmic". If that is what the evidence tells you, it is incumbent on you not to inflict that on the country you govern.

Until recently, markets continued to react as if something must turn up and on the basis that "no deal" was a virtually unimaginable scenario. That risk has therefore been seriously under priced for a year or more, because we are dealing with a political generation which has no serious experience of bad times and is frankly cavalier about precipitating events they cannot then control, but feel they might exploit.

Nothing is more redolent of the pre-First World War era, when few believed that a very long period of European peace and equilibrium could be shattered in months.

8TH LESSON:

You cannot, and should not want to, conduct such a huge negotiation as untransparently as the UK has. And in the end, it does you no good to try.

At virtually every stage in this negotiation, the EU side has deployed transparency, whether on its position papers, its graphic presentations of its take on viable options and parameters, or its "no deal" notices to the private sector to dictate the terms of the debate and shape the outcome.

A secretive, opaque British government, hampered in fairness by being permanently divided against itself and therefore largely unable to articulate any agreed, coherent position, has floundered in its wake.

It is a rather unusual experience for the EU – always portrayed as a bunch of wildly out of touch technocrats producing turgid, jargon-ridden Eurocrat prose up against "genuine" politicians who speak "human" – to win propaganda battles. Let alone win them this easily.

But, frankly, bruising experiences over recent decades – as it has had to cope with demands for vastly greater transparency in its conduct of trade policy (which has moved from being the theatre of technocrat nerds to being the hottest topic on the planet, precisely, as I say, because trade negotiations cut to the heart of sovereignty and identity questions as soon as they encroach on "domestic" regulation) – have forced Brussels to up its game.

Failure to do so would have meant losing all

public support for driving trade liberalisation and signing trade deals – which, whether UK politicians wish to believe it or not, is what the EU does more of than any other trade bloc on the planet at the moment.

No government or trade bloc has any chance of doing deals with Japan, Canada, the US or Mercosur – or indeed, the UK when that moment comes – unless it can explain comprehensibly to its public what is in it for them.

The battle for free trade policies – always difficult in the US – has, after all, gone rather convincingly backwards in both major US parties in the last 20 years. I am tempted to say it's only much of the Tory Eurosceptic Americanophile establishment which appears not quite to have noticed that, and seems to view President's Trump's administration as more of a bastion of free trade than it seems to the rest of the world.

Those here who most often advocate our

leaving the EU "on WTO terms", viewing it as the strong guardian of a rules-based liberal international trading order and a forum in which the UK can play a leadership role in making progress towards freer global trade, do not seem to be paying too close attention to how senior Republicans view its function and record. The closest analogue to the way the American Right views the WTO dispute settlement regime is how the UK Right views the European Court of Justice: a supranational affront to sovereignty.

To be clear, this is not to argue that by applying lipstick to the pig of the Chequers proposal, or the Prime Minister's proposed deal, the course of history would have been changed. You can't redeem a bad deal by advertising on Facebook.

Rather, that the negotiation process, politically, in and beyond Parliament, had to be different from the outset. And it will have to be different at the next stage. You can't possibly run one of the largest and most complex trade negotiations on the planet and leave most supposed insiders, let alone a much wider public, in the dark about the extremely difficult choices they will face.

At extremely sensitive stages, negotiators of course have to disappear into a "tunnel", to have any safe space in which to explore potential landing zones. That is inevitable.

But this government has repeatedly failed to explain to a wider audience what the real constraints and trade-offs are in arriving at the sort of landing zone the Prime Minister views as some combination of desirable and unavoidable.

9TH LESSON:

**Real honesty with the public is the best –
the only – policy if we are to get to the other
side of Brexit with a healthy democracy, a
reasonably unified country and a strong
economy.**

The debate of the last 30 months has suffered
from opacity, delusion-mongering and men-
dacity on all sides.

The Prime Minister's call for opponents of
her deal to "be honest" and not simply wish
away intractable problems like the backstop,
which was always, and will remain, a central

question in any resolution of the issue, is reasonable enough.

I have talked briefly already of the quite extraordinary "cakeism" in the various options in the table.

At the extremes we have the "no dealers" quite happy to jump off the cliff, lying openly about the extent to which WTO rules would provide a safety net if we did, and producing fantasy "managed no deal" options which will not fly for the reasons I have set out.

And then there are the "people's voters". I confess I deplore the term itself: they want a second referendum with "remain" on the ballot – for which one can make a case, given the dismal place we have now ended up, and given possible Parliamentary paralysis – but must surely understand the huge further alienation that this would engender amongst those who will think that, yet again, their views are being ignored until they conform.

One still hears Shadow Cabinet Members promising, with a straight face, that, even after a General Election they want to force, there would be time for Labour to negotiate a completely different deal – *including* a full trade deal, which would replicate all the advantages of the Single Market and Customs Union. And all within weeks because much more flexibility would suddenly be forthcoming from the EU side. I assume they haven't yet stopped laughing in Brussels.

Too much of our current political debate just insults people's intelligence and suggests that every facet of Brexit you don't like is purely a feature of the Prime Minister's version of it, rather than intrinsic to leaving.

I dislike plenty of the Prime Minister's deal. It's obviously a bad deal. But given her own views and preferences, her bitterly divided party and the negotiating realities with the other side of the table, I can at least understand that she is on pretty much the only landing zone she could ever conceivably reach.

Those aspiring to a radically different one owe us honest accounts, not pipe dreams, of how they propose to get there, and the time scale over which they will.

But the dishonesty of the debate has, I am afraid, been fuelled by the government for the last two and a half years.

It took ages before grudging recognition was given to the reality that no trade deal – even an embryonic one – would be struck before exit, and that no trade deals with other players would be in place either.

Even now, the Prime Minister still talks publicly about the Political Declaration as if it defines the future relationship with some degree of precision, and defines it largely in line with her own Chequers proposal, when it simply does neither.

It is vague to the point of vacuity in many

places, strewn with adjectives and studiously ambiguous in a way that enables it to be sold as offering something to all, without committing anyone fully to anything.

Any number of different final destinations are accommodable within this text, which was precisely the thinking in drafting it, to maximise the chances of it being voted through, when all the EU side was really determined to nail now was within the Withdrawal Treaty: rights, money and the backstop.

For the same reason – the desperate inability to acknowledge that it was going to take very many years to get to the other side of the Brexit process – we have had the bizarre euphemism of the "implementation period" after March 2019, when there is nothing to "implement", and everything still to negotiate.

I dislike the "vassal state" terminology, but anyone can see the democratic problem with being subject to laws made in rooms where no Brit was present and living under a court's jurisdiction where there is no British judge.

And if we are to avoid the backstop coming into force, we are now going to end up prolonging the transition, because the FTA won't be done by the end of 2020, and the EU well knows that the UK won't be keen on cliff jumping in the run up to an election.

We have had the several bizarre contortions over trying to invent a customs proposal which enabled us to escape the Common External Tariff (which applies to Customs Union members) but still derive all the advantages of a quasi Customs Union. Even the "all UK" backstop proposal, which was the Prime Minister's own proposal to avoid the potential advent of a Northern Ireland-specific backstop intolerable to her Democratic Unionist allies, has ended up being called a temporary "Arrangement" when we all actually know it to be a temporary Union, as nothing else could fly under WTO rules. But the "U" word is too toxic for polite company evidently.

On the backstop itself, it was obvious, reading the December 2017 Agreement document from outside government, that this must lead inexorably to where we have now reached.

There was no other endgame from that point. Which was why, a year ago, I started telling corporates they were really seriously underestimating the chances of a "no deal" outcome.

Still, we got sophistry, evasions, euphemisms and sometimes straight denials at home, whilst in the EU, the PM and senior ministers several times appeared to be backsliding on clear commitments as soon as they saw draft legal texts giving effect to agreements they had struck.

That deepened the distrust and if anything hardened the EU's resolve to nail the backstop issue down legally. And, from the apoplectic reaction to the Attorney General's advice which elegantly stated the totally obvious – that there could be no unilateral right for the UK to terminate the backstop whenever it chose, regardless of whether there was something to replace it – you can now rather see why.

There is no point in my speculating here precisely on what might finally get manufactured by the EU, or on its exact legal force. Brussels is always very adroit at such exercises in solemnly re-framing things which have already been agreed in ways that make the medicine slip down.

But however they re-emphasise their intention, which I believe, that the backstop should not be permanent, it is the very existence of it in conjunction with the cliff edge which will dictate the shape of the trade negotiations.

We may well now be beyond the point at which any solely clarifying Declaration or Decision can sell.

And if we are, it's largely because the whole

conduct of the negotiation has further burned through trust in the political class.

That, in my view, should force a fundamental rethink of how the next phase is conducted – whether this deal staggers, with some clarification, across the line in several weeks' time and we go into the next phase with the cards stacked, or whether we have a new Prime Minister who attempts to reset direction, but will find, as I say, that regardless of what reset they attempt, rather a lot of the negotiating dynamics and parameters remain completely unchanged.

Either way, my final lesson is that we shall need a radically different method and style if the country is to heal and unify behind some proposed destination.

And that requires leadership which is far more honest in setting out the fundamental choices still ahead – the difficult trade-offs between sovereignty and national control and keeping market access for our goods and services in our biggest market – and which sets out to build at least some viable consensus.

I would like to end with a quote which seems to me to be particularly appropriate on this day, at this time. This famous speech is made by a king who has gained power, still holds it, but whose enemies are now openly attacking him. He can no longer find meaning in the success he has won, or even in life itself. In a compelling image he speaks of life, and in particular of the part he has played in life as: "a walking shadow, a poor player that struts and frets his time upon the stage. It is a tale, told by an idiot, full of sound and fury, signifying nothing."

The time to lose ourselves in stories has ended. Our politicians can no longer get away with strutting and fretting or with sound and fury. It's time to wake up from the dream and face the facts.

ACKNOWLEDGEMENTS

I owe particular thanks to Dame Janet Beer, Vice Chancellor of Liverpool University, and Professor Mark Boyle, Director of the Heseltine Institute at the University, and their great colleagues, for inviting and for hosting me so generously for the lecture on which this essay is based.

I am hugely grateful to all my old friends and colleagues, particularly at the UK Permanent Representation in Brussels and in the Cabinet Office, who taught me virtually all I know about the EU, and put up with my endless stupid questions and even more endless e-mails.

I owe a particular debt to the late David Bostock, who taught me that, with the EU, on which his expertise was unrivalled, unless you fully got to the grips with the process, you would be totally lost on the substance. That lesson stayed with me in every international negotiation I tried to conduct as an official.

Above all, I owe everything to my wife, Steph, and to Ben and Ellie, who have been wonderful companions and inspirations through everything, and have had to put up with talk about Brexit since well before the rest of the world heard the term.